Bolognese Pasta

Ingredients

1 tbsp olive oil
4 rashers smoked streaky bacon, finely chopped
2 medium onions, finely chopped
2 carrots, trimmed and finely chopped
2 celery sticks, finely chopped
2 garlic cloves, finely chopped
2-3 sprigs rosemary leaves, picked and finely chopped
500g beef mince

Instructions for preparing pasta bolognese:

Heat the olive oil in a large saucepan over medium heat. Add the chopped bacon and cook for 2-3 minutes until the bacon is crispy and has released its fat.

Add the chopped onions, carrots, celery, and garlic to the pan. Cook for 5-7 minutes, stirring occasionally, until the vegetables have softened and are translucent.

Stir in the rosemary and cook for an additional minute.

Add the beef mince to the pan and cook until browned, breaking it up with a wooden spoon as it cooks.

Once the beef mince is browned, add your preferred seasonings, such as salt, pepper, and dried oregano.

Pour in enough water or stock to cover the mixture, and bring it to a boil. Reduce the heat to low and let it simmer for 30 minutes, or until the sauce has thickened and the flavors have developed.

Cook your favorite pasta according to the instructions on the package, then drain it and return it to the pan.

Stir the sauce into the pasta and cook for a minute or two to combine. Serve the pasta bolognese with grated Parmesan cheese and freshly chopped parsley, if desired. Enjoy!

This cookbook contains healthy recipes for the whole family that are easy to make and budget friendly. Whether you're looking for some healthy snacks or a delicious main course, this book has it all! You can find many healthy dishes with simple ingredients, low-budget options, and meals that come together in no time. With these recipes, everyone in the family is sure to find something that satisfies their taste buds. Get the cookbook today and start cooking healthy and delicious meals for your loved ones!

Happy cooking!

Air Fryer Chicken Meatballs

Into a large mixing bowl, add ground chicken, egg, bread crumbs, parmesan cheese, salt, pepper, garlic powder, onion powder, paprika, olive oil and parsley and mix until combined. No, take a heaping tablespoon from the chicken mixture and shape it into a ball.

Next, place the chicken meatballs in the air fryer basket and set to 375°F for 12-15 minutes flipping halfway through. This healthy recipe is an easy and fast way to make delicious, low budget meals! You can top these chicken meatballs over pasta or a salad for a complete meal. With air frying, you don't have to worry about the oil or the mess. No need to stand over a hot stove, just preheat and enjoy healthy eating in no time! You can also try this recipe with ground turkey or beef for even more delicious variations. Air frying has revolutionized healthy cooking; easy, fast and healthy recipes are now achievable at home without sacrificing taste. Try this easy air fryer chicken meatballs recipe and enjoy healthy eating today!

The end result: delicious, healthy air fryer chicken meatballs that are an easy and fast way to make low budget meals. With just a few ingredients and the air fryer, you can have healthy meals on the table in no time. Enjoy!

Chicken Rice

Ingredients

¼ cup sesame oil
2 tablespoons chicken fat, chopped
2 cloves garlic, minced
1 tablespoon fresh ginger, minced
1 teaspoon kosher salt
2 cups long grain rice, rinsed and drained
2 cups reserved chicken spawning broth

Instructions for preparing Chicken Rice:

Heat the sesame oil in a medium saucepan over medium heat. Add the chicken fat, garlic, and ginger and cook until fragrant, about 2 minutes.

Stir in the kosher salt and the rice and cook, stirring, for 2 minutes.

Pour in the reserved chicken spawning broth and bring to a boil. Reduce the heat to low, cover the saucepan with a tight-fitting lid, and simmer for 18-20 minutes, or until the liquid has been absorbed and the rice is cooked through.

Remove the saucepan from heat and let it sit, covered, for 10 minutes. Fluff the rice with a fork, then serve with the cooked chicken.

Enjoy your delicious Chicken Rice!

Chicken Parmigiana:

Ingredients for

2 large, skinless chicken breasts, halved through the middle
2 eggs, beaten
75g breadcrumbs
75g parmesan, grated
1 tbsp olive oil
2 garlic cloves, crushed
Half a 690ml jar of passata
1 tsp caster sugar

Instructions for preparing Chicken Parmigiana:

Preheat the oven to 200°C (400°F). Line a baking sheet with parchment paper.

Place the beaten eggs in a shallow dish and set aside. In another shallow dish, mix together the breadcrumbs and grated parmesan.

Dip each chicken breast into the beaten eggs, then coat with the breadcrumb mixture, pressing the breadcrumbs firmly onto the chicken.

Heat the olive oil in a large skillet over medium heat. Add the coated chicken breasts and cook until browned on both sides, about 3-5 minutes per side.

Transfer the chicken to the prepared baking sheet and bake in the preheated oven for 15-20 minutes, or until the chicken is cooked through and the breadcrumbs are golden brown.

While the chicken is baking, prepare the sauce. In a small saucepan, heat the garlic in the remaining olive oil until fragrant. Stir in the passata and caster sugar and cook until heated through.

Serve the chicken parmigiana topped with the warm tomato sauce, with a side of pasta or vegetables, if desired. Enjoy!

Pulled Chicken Salad

Ingredients

1 small roasted chicken, about 1kg
½ red cabbage, cored and finely sliced
3 carrots, coarsely grated or finely shredded
5 spring onions, finely sliced on the diagonal
2 red chillies, halved and thinly sliced
A small bunch of coriander, roughly chopped, including stalks

Instructions for preparing Pulled Chicken Salad:

Remove the meat from the roasted chicken and shred it into bite-sized pieces using two forks or your hands.

In a large bowl, mix together the shredded chicken, finely sliced red cabbage, grated carrots, finely sliced spring onions, thinly sliced red chillies, and chopped coriander.

Season the salad with salt and pepper, to taste.

To serve, arrange the salad on a large platter or divide it evenly onto individual plates. You can also drizzle some vinaigrette or your favorite dressing over the salad, if desired.

Serve the Pulled Chicken Salad immediately and enjoy!

Healthy Salmon Pasta

Ingredients

8 ounces spaghetti or other pasta, uncooked
1/2 pound fresh salmon
1/4 teaspoon onion powder
Salt & pepper, to taste
1 tablespoon olive oil
1 tablespoon butter
1 tablespoon flour
3 cloves garlic, minced

Instructions for preparing Healthy Salmon Pasta:

Cook the spaghetti or other pasta according to the package directions. Reserve 1/2 cup of the pasta cooking water and drain the rest.

Cut the salmon into 1-inch pieces and season with onion powder, salt, and pepper.

In a large skillet, heat the olive oil over medium heat. Add the seasoned salmon and cook until just browned on the outside, about 2-3 minutes per side. Remove the salmon from the skillet and set aside.

In the same skillet, melt the butter over medium heat. Whisk in the flour until smooth and cook for 1 minute, or until the mixture starts to turn golden brown.

Stir in the minced garlic and cook for an additional minute, or until fragrant. Gradually whisk in the reserved pasta cooking water until the sauce is smooth.

Add the cooked salmon back into the skillet and stir to coat with the sauce. Cook for 2-3 minutes, or until the salmon is cooked through.

Toss the cooked pasta with the salmon sauce in the skillet. Serve immediately, garnished with chopped parsley or other herbs, if desired.

Enjoy your delicious and healthy Salmon Pasta!

Potato Soup

Ingredients

8 slices thin bacon, cut into 1-inch pieces
1 medium onion, diced
2 medium carrots, scrubbed clean and diced
2 stalks celery, diced
4 small russet potatoes, peeled and diced
8 cups low-sodium chicken or vegetable broth
3 tablespoons all-purpose flour
1 cup milk

Instructions for preparing Potato Soup:

In a large pot, cook the bacon over medium heat until crispy, about 5-7 minutes. Remove the bacon with a slotted spoon and set aside. Reserve 2 tablespoons of the bacon fat in the pot.

Add the diced onion, carrots, and celery to the pot and cook until the vegetables are soft and the onion is translucent, about 5-7 minutes.

Stir in the diced potatoes and the chicken or vegetable broth. Bring the soup to a boil, then reduce the heat and simmer until the potatoes are tender, about 20-25 minutes.

In a separate bowl, whisk together the flour and milk until smooth. Stir the flour mixture into the soup and cook until the soup has thickened, about 5-7 minutes.

Return the cooked bacon to the pot and stir to combine. Season the soup with salt and pepper, to taste.

Serve the soup hot, garnished with freshly chopped parsley or green onions, if desired.

Enjoy your delicious and comforting Potato Soup!

Potato Broccoli Frittata

Ingredients for 6 Servings

1 1/2 cups cubed potatoes
2 cups coarsely chopped broccoli florets
1 tablespoon olive oil
1/2 cup coarsely chopped onion
1 teaspoon McCormick Oregano Leaves
1 teaspoon McCormick Whole Rosemary Leaves, finely crushed
1 teaspoon McCormick Whole Thyme Leaves
8 large eggs
1/4 teaspoon salt
1/4 teaspoon black pepper
1/4 cup grated Parmesan cheese

Instructions for preparing Potato and Broccoli Frittata:

Preheat oven to 400°F. In a large skillet, heat the olive oil over medium heat. Add the potatoes, broccoli, onion, oregano, rosemary, and thyme. Cook for 10 to 12 minutes or until the vegetables are tender and lightly browned, stirring occasionally.

In a large bowl, whisk the eggs, salt, pepper, and Parmesan cheese together until well combined. Stir in the cooked vegetable mixture.

Pour the egg mixture back into the skillet. Cook over medium heat until the bottom is set and the top is almost set, about 5 minutes.

Place the skillet in the oven and bake for 10 minutes or until the frittata is set and lightly browned on top.

Remove the frittata from the oven and let it cool for 5 minutes. Slide the frittata onto a serving platter and cut into wedges.

Enjoy your delicious and nutritious Potato and Broccoli Frittata! Serve it warm or at room temperature, as a tasty and complete meal.

Black Bean Enchiladas

Ingredients (6 Servings):

1 tablespoon olive oil
2 cloves garlic, minced
1 large green bell pepper, diced
1 small onion, diced
1 (15-oz) can BUSH'S black beans, drained and rinsed
1 (15-oz) can yellow corn, drained and rinsed
1 teaspoon kosher salt, plus more to taste
1/2 teaspoon ground cumin
1 cup enchilada sauce, divided
8 (6-inch) corn tortillas
1 cup shredded Monterey Jack cheese
Fresh cilantro, chopped (optional)
Sour cream and diced avocado, for serving (optional)

Instructions for preparing Black Bean Enchiladas:

Preheat oven to 375°F. In a large skillet, heat the olive oil over medium heat. Add the garlic, bell pepper, and onion and cook until the vegetables are tender, about 5 minutes.

Add the black beans, corn, salt, and cumin to the skillet and cook until heated through, about 2 minutes. Remove from heat.

Spread 1/4 cup of the enchilada sauce in the bottom of a 9x13 inch baking dish.

Place a tortilla on a flat surface and spoon a generous amount of the black bean mixture down the center of the tortilla. Roll up the tortilla and place it seam side down in the baking dish. Repeat with the remaining tortillas.

Pour the remaining enchilada sauce over the top of the rolled tortillas. Sprinkle the shredded cheese on top.

Cover the dish with foil and bake for 20 minutes. Remove the foil and continue to bake until the cheese is melted and bubbly, about 5-10 minutes.

Let the enchiladas cool for a few minutes before serving. Garnish with fresh cilantro, if desired. Serve with sour cream and diced avocado on the side, if desired.

Enjoy your delicious and flavorful Black Bean Enchiladas!

Creamy Tomato Soup

Tomato Soup is a great lunch choice for kids because it's easy to make and packed with healthy ingredients. Plus, they will love the bright and vibrant colour! Here's what you'll need to make this delicious tomato soup recipe:

- 1-1.25kg/2lb 4oz-2lb 12oz ripe tomatoes

- 1 medium onion

- 1 small carrot

- 1 celery stick

- 2 tbsp olive oil

- 2 squirts of tomato purée (about 2 tsp)

- A good pinch of sugar

- 2 bay leaves

Once you've gathered all the ingredients, it's time to start cooking! Begin by heating the olive oil in a large saucepan and adding the diced onion, carrot, celery stick. Cook over medium heat for about 5 minutes until softened. Then add the tomatoes, purée, bay leaves and sugar. Cover with a lid and cook for 40 minutes. Once the soup is cooked, remove the bay leaves and blend until smooth with a blender.

Serve up this delicious tomato soup with some crusty bread or croutons on top and you have an easy, healthy lunch that your kids will love! Enjoy!

Salmon Burger

Ingredients

1½ pounds skinless, boneless salmon.
2 teaspoons Dijon mustard.
2 shallots, peeled and cut into chunks.
½ cup coarse bread crumbs.
1 tablespoon capers, drained.
Salt and black pepper.
2 tablespoons butter or olive oil.
Lemon wedges.

With all the necessary ingredients in hand, you can easily prepare a nutritious and delicious salmon burger lunch for your kids. Begin by preheating the oven to 350 degrees Fahrenheit. Then place the salmon in a food processor and process until it becomes somewhat smooth. Add mustard, shallots, bread crumbs, capers, salt, and pepper, and process until everything is combined.

Form the mixture into four patties and place on a greased baking sheet. Bake in preheated oven for 20 minutes, flipping the burgers halfway through cooking time. When done, remove from oven and heat butter or oil in a large skillet over medium heat. Place salmon burgers in skillet cook for 3 to 4 minutes per side. Serve with a lemon wedge, and enjoy! The perfect healthy lunch recipe for kids!

This salmon burger recipe is sure to please even the pickiest eaters. Not only is it delicious, but it's also a great way to incorporate nutrient-rich fish into your family's meals. With just a few simple steps, you can easily prepare a nutritious and filling lunch in no time! Try this salmon burger recipe today and enjoy the deliciousness.

Shrimp Pasta

Ingredients

8 ounces fettuccine.
1 pound medium shrimp, peeled and deveined.
Kosher salt and freshly ground black pepper, to taste.
8 tablespoons 1 stick unsalted butter, divided.
4 cloves garlic, minced.
½ teaspoon dried oregano.
½ teaspoon crushed red pepper flakes.
2 cups baby arugula.

Shrimp Pasta is a healthy and easy dinner for kids that you can whip up in no time. To prepare it, start by bringing a large pot of salted water to a boil over high heat. Once boiling, add the fettuccine and cook until al dente according to package directions. Drain pasta into a colander and set aside.

Meanwhile, in a large skillet over medium heat, melt 4 tablespoons of butter. Add the shrimp and season with salt and pepper to taste. Cook, stirring occasionally until pink and cooked through, about 3-4 minutes; set aside.

To the same skillet add remaining butter, garlic, oregano and red pepper flakes. Cook, stirring frequently, until fragrant, about 1-2 minutes. Stir in the cooked pasta and shrimp; season with salt and pepper to taste.

Finally, stir in the arugula until wilted, about 1 minute. Serve immediately, garnished with more red pepper flakes if desired. Enjoy!

Vegetable Pizza

Vegetarian pizza is a flavorful and healthy option for kids that's simple to prepare. There are so many vegetarian pizza toppings available, it's easy to create unique recipes that appeal to the whole family.

To make vegetarian pizza, start by preheating your oven according to the instructions on the package of store-bought or homemade pizza dough. Next, select your favorite vegetarian toppings. Tomatoes, onions, arugula, kale, eggplants, bell peppers, spinach, zucchini and mushrooms all make wonderful vegetarian topping choices. For even more flavor you can add in some cooked or roasted vegetables such as olives or artichoke hearts. Spread your selected toppings over the prepared crust and top with your desired amount of cheese.

Bake the vegetarian pizza in the oven according to the dough packaging instructions and enjoy! Vegetarian pizzas are a great way to provide kids with healthy vegetarian recipes that they can enjoy. Experiment with different types of vegetables, cheeses and seasonings to create vegetarian recipes for kids that everyone will love. With just a few simple steps you can have a delicious vegetarian pizza ready to eat in no time!

Mac And Cheese

Macaroni and Cheese is a healthy and delicious pasta dish that can be easily prepared at home. To make it, you will need 8 ounces of uncooked elbow macaroni (Great Value Elbows, 48 oz.), ¼ cup salted butter, 3 tablespoons all-purpose flour, 2 ½ cups milk, or more as needed, 2 cups shredded sharp Cheddar cheese, ½ cup finely grated Parmesan cheese, and salt and ground black pepper to taste (optional).

To begin, preheat your oven to 350 degrees Fahrenheit. Bring a large pot of salted water to a boil over high heat. Once boiling, add the elbow macaroni and cook until al dente, according to package instructions. Once cooked, drain the macaroni and set aside.

Meanwhile, in a large saucepan over medium heat melt the butter and stir in the flour until combined. Gradually whisk in the milk a little at a time until all of it is incorporated and there are no lumps left. Allow the sauce to simmer until it thickens, stirring constantly.

Once the sauce has thickened, turn off the heat and stir in the Cheddar and Parmesan cheeses until melted. Season with salt and black pepper (optional). Gradually stir in the cooked macaroni until everything is coated with cheese sauce.

Transfer the macaroni and cheese to a greased 9x13 inch baking dish. Bake in preheated oven for about 30 minutes, or until the cheese is nice and bubbly. Serve warm and enjoy!

The delicious healthy pasta dish of Macaroni and Cheese can easily be prepared at home with just a few simple ingredients. Enjoy this creamy and cheesy dish year-round!

Cheesy Broccoli Pasta

Ingredients
½ cup butter.
1 onion, chopped. Fresh Onions.
1 (16 ounce) package frozen chopped broccoli.
4 (14.5 ounce) cans chicken broth.
1 (1 pound) loaf processed cheese food, cubed.
2 cups milk.
1 tablespoon garlic powder.
⅔ cup cornstarch.

This delicious cheesy broccoli pasta is a sure hit for kids and adults alike! With just a few simple steps, anyone can make this delicious dish in no time.

First, melt the butter in a large pot over medium heat. Add the chopped onion and cook until softened, about 5 minutes. Next, add the frozen chopped broccoli and chicken broth and bring to a boil. Reduce the heat, cover, and simmer for 15 minutes.

Once done, add the cubed cheese food, milk, garlic powder and cornstarch to the pot. Give it all a good stir then cover and cook for about 10 more minutes or until the sauce has thickened. Serve hot with your favorite sides!

This cheesy broccoli pasta is delicious and easy to make, making it an ideal recipe for kids. If you're looking for a delicious and nutritious dish that your whole family can enjoy, this is the perfect choice! So what are you waiting for? Try out this delicious cheesy broccoli pasta today!

Enjoy

Chicken Avocado Rolls

Ingredients

1 cup cooked chicken breast diced or shredded.
1 avocado, pitted and diced.
1/4 cup shredded cheese or choice.
1/4 cup diced tomato.
2 tablespoons onion minced (optional)
2 tablespoons cilantro minced.
2 tablespoons sour-cream or Greek yogurt.
1 tablespoon lime juice.

Chicken avocado rolls are the perfect healthy lunch option for your kids. With only a few simple ingredients, you can easily put together this delicious and nutritious meal in no time! Start with 1 cup of cooked chicken breast diced or shredded. Then add one diced avocado, 1/4 cup of shredded cheese (or whatever type you prefer), 1/4 cup of diced tomato, 2 tablespoons of minced onion (optional), 2 tablespoons of minced cilantro, 2 tablespoons of sour-cream or Greek yogurt and 1 tablespoon of lime juice. Mix it all together and spoon the mixture into some lettuce leaves to make your chicken avocado rolls! Serve them up with a side salad or some steamed veggies for extra nutrition. Your kids will love them!

Salmon And Cream Cheese Sandwich

Ingredients
Bread. ...
Whipped Cream Cheese. ...
Smoked Salmon. ...
Fresh Chives. ...
Fresh Parsley. ...
Salt and Black Pepper.

This easy-to-make sandwich is a great way to introduce kids to the delicious flavors of smoked salmon! Start by taking two slices of whole wheat bread and spreading a generous layer of whipped cream cheese on one side. Layer on some thinly sliced smoked salmon, and top with fresh chives, parsley, salt and black pepper for flavor. Serve up with a side of fruit for a healthy, delicious and fun lunch that the kids will love! Enjoy!

Spinach And Feta Pie

INGREDIENTS
400 G (14 OZ) SPINACH LEAVES, FRESH OR FROZEN.
FRESH NUTMEG.
SEA SALT AND FRESHLY GROUND PEPPER.
200 G (7 OZ) FETA.
SQUEEZE OF LEMON JUICE.
3-4 LARGE SHEETS OF READY-ROLLED PUFF PASTRY (PREFERABLY MADE WITH BUTTER)
1 EGG BEATEN WITH A DASH OF MILK FOR THE EGG WASH.

Spinach and feta pie is a healthy, low-budget recipe that is easy and fast to make. This savory dish consists of 400 grams (14 oz) of fresh or frozen spinach leaves, fresh nutmeg, sea salt, freshly ground pepper, 200 grams (7 oz) of feta cheese and a squeeze of lemon juice. To top it off, you'll need 3-4 large sheets of ready-rolled puff pastry (preferably made with butter). Once the ingredients are prepared, simply assemble and brush your pie with an egg wash beaten with a dash of milk. Then bake for 25 minutes or until golden brown in a preheated oven. You can serve this healthy and delicious pie as an appetizer, side dish or even main course. Enjoy!

Chicken Noodles

Chicken Noodle Stir Fry is a healthy, low budget recipe that is easy and fast to make. It only needs a few simple ingredients: 2 nests dried egg noodles, 1 tbsp sesame oil, 3 skinless boneless chicken thighs cut into strips, 3 tbsp soy sauce, 2 tbsp honey, 1 tbsp vegetable oil, 1 garlic clove peeled and finely sliced, and 3cm piece ginger peeled and cut into matchsticks. This recipe is perfect for a healthy, quick meal that won't break your budget. To get started, simply heat the vegetable oil in a large frying pan over medium-high heat. Add the chicken strips and stir fry until golden brown. Then add the garlic, ginger, soy sauce, honey and sesame oil and stir fry for a further minute until fragrant. Finally, add the egg noodles and cook until just heated through. Serve with steamed vegetables or your favorite side dish for a healthy and delicious meal in no time! Enjoy!

This recipe is sure to become one of your favorites - healthy, easy and fast to make, and cost effective. Give it a try today!

Note: Be sure to adjust the ingredients to meet your dietary needs and preferences. For example, if you're vegetarian or vegan, substitute the chicken for your favorite veggies! If you prefer gluten-free noodles, use gluten free egg noodles instead.

Happy cooking!

Roasted Black Bean Burger

Ingredients

1½ red onions.
200 g mixed mushrooms.
100 g rye bread.
ground coriander.
1 x 400 g tin of black beans.
40 g mature Cheddar cheese.
4 soft rolls.
100 g ripe cherry tomatoes.

Instructions

Preheat the oven to 200°C (180°C fan) / 400°F / Gas Mark 6. Line a baking sheet with parchment paper.

Chop the red onions and mushrooms into small pieces and roast them on the prepared baking sheet for 10-15 minutes or until they are soft and lightly browned.

Cut the rye bread into small cubes and place in a large bowl.

Drain and rinse the black beans and add them to the bowl with the bread cubes.

Grate the Cheddar cheese and add it to the bowl with the bread and beans.

Add the roasted onions and mushrooms to the bowl, along with 2 teaspoons of ground coriander.

Mash the mixture together using a fork or potato masher, until it forms a sticky, cohesive mixture.

Divide the mixture into 4 portions and form each portion into a patty.

Place the patties on the prepared baking sheet and bake in the preheated oven for 15-20 minutes, or until they are firm and crispy.

While the burgers are baking, slice the soft rolls and halve the cherry tomatoes.

Once the burgers are cooked, assemble the sandwiches by placing a patty in each roll and topping with cherry tomato slices. Serve immediately. Enjoy!

Vegetable Beef Soup

Ingredients

Beef stew meat
Olive oil
Yellow onion
Carrots
Celery
Garlic
Canned tomatoes
Low-sodium beef broth or chicken broth
Dried herbs - basil, oregano, and thyme
Salt and pepper
Red potatoes
Green beans
Frozen corn and peas
Fresh parsley

If you're looking for a delicious and healthy lunch option for your kids, this Vegetable Beef Soup is perfect! It's packed with protein-rich beef, vegetables, and herbs that will give them the nutrition they need. Plus, it's easy to make - just throw all of the ingredients into a pot and let it simmer until the vegetables are tender and the beef is cooked through. For a heartier soup, add red potatoes and green beans. To make it even more nutritious, include frozen corn and peas as well as fresh parsley. Serve with a side salad or crusty bread for a satisfying meal! Enjoy!

With this Vegetable Beef Soup, you can be sure that your kids are getting a nutritious and delicious lunch with plenty of protein, vitamins, and minerals. Not only is it good for them, but it's also easy to make and can be prepared ahead of time. Plus, the leftovers can easily be reheated for another meal! Enjoy!

Beefy Macaroni And Cheese

Ingredients

3/4 pound ground beef (90% lean)
1 1/2 cups water.
1 cup macaroni, uncooked.
1 can diced tomatoes, canned, undrained.
7 Servings Eating Smart Seasoning Mix (1/2 cup or 8 Tablespoons)
1/2 cup shredded cheese.
salt (optional, to taste)

Kids will love this delicious and nutritious beefy macaroni and cheese! This one-dish meal is a cinch to prepare, with only seven ingredients. Start by browning the ground beef in a large saucepan over medium heat. Once the meat is cooked through, add the water, macaroni, tomatoes, and Eating Smart Seasoning Mix, and bring to a boil. Reduce the heat to low, cover, and simmer for 12-15 minutes or until the macaroni is tender. Stir in the cheese and season with salt if desired. Serve it up as a warm dinner on colder days, or let cool slightly and pack it for lunch! The leftovers are great too, so don't be afraid to make a larger batch. Enjoy!

Spinach Pancakes

Ingredients

125g self-raising flour.
1 tsp baking powder.
½ tbsp sugar (any kind)
2 eggs.
1 tbsp melted butter, plus extra for frying.
100ml milk.
50g baby spinach leaves, washed and chopped.
berries and maple syrup, to serve.

Instructions

In a large bowl, whisk together the self-raising flour, baking powder, and sugar.

In a separate bowl, whisk the eggs and add in the melted butter and milk.

Add the wet ingredients to the dry ingredients and whisk until just combined.

Stir in the chopped baby spinach leaves.

Heat a non-stick frying pan over medium heat and add a small amount of butter.

Using a 1/4 cup measure, pour the batter into the pan and spread it out into a circle. Cook for 2-3 minutes on each side, or until the pancakes are golden brown and cooked through.

Repeat the process with the remaining batter, adding more butter to the pan as needed.

Serve the pancakes warm with a dollop of Greek yogurt, fresh berries, and a drizzle of maple syrup. Enjoy!

Tofu Fried Rice

Ingredients

2 cups uncooked instant rice.
2 tablespoons vegetable oil, divided.
1 (14-ounce) package reduced-fat firm tofu, drained and cut into (1/2-inch) cubes.
2 large eggs, lightly beaten.
1 cup (1/2-inch-thick) slices green onions.
1 cup frozen peas and carrots, thawed.
4 garlic cloves, minced.

Instructions

Cook the instant rice according to the package instructions and set aside.

In a large non-stick pan or wok, heat 1 tablespoon of vegetable oil over medium heat. Add the tofu cubes and cook for 4-5 minutes, or until they are lightly browned. Remove from the pan and set aside.

In the same pan, heat the remaining 1 tablespoon of oil. Add the beaten eggs and cook, stirring frequently, for 2-3 minutes, or until the eggs are scrambled and set. Remove from the pan and set aside.

Add the green onions, peas and carrots, and garlic to the pan and cook for 2-3 minutes, or until the vegetables are tender.

Add the cooked rice to the pan and stir to combine with the vegetables. Cook for 2-3 minutes, or until the rice is heated through.

Add the cooked tofu and scrambled eggs to the pan and stir to combine. Cook for a further minute to heat through.

Serve hot, garnished with additional green onions if desired.
Enjoy!

Chickpea Chard Pork

Ingredients

400 g piece of higher-welfare pork fillet.
1 x 480 g jar of roasted peeled peppers in brine.
300 g rainbow chard.
1 heaped teaspoon fennel seeds.
1 x 660 g jar of chickpeas.

Instructions

Preheat the oven to 200°C (180°C fan) / 400°F / Gas Mark 6.

Cut the pork fillet into 1 inch thick slices and season with salt and pepper.
Heat a large ovenproof pan over medium-high heat and add a drizzle of oil. Sear the pork slices for 2-3 minutes on each side, or until they are golden brown. Remove from the pan and set aside.
Drain the jar of roasted peppers and chop into bite-sized pieces. Set aside.
Wash and chop the rainbow chard, discarding the tough stems.
In the same pan, add the fennel seeds and cook for 1-2 minutes, or until fragrant.
Drain and rinse the chickpeas and add to the pan with the fennel seeds. Cook for 2-3 minutes, or until heated through.
Add the chopped chard to the pan and stir to combine with the chickpeas. Cook for 2-3 minutes, or until the chard is wilted.
Return the pork slices to the pan and spoon the chickpea and chard mixture over the pork.
Add the chopped roasted peppers to the pan and place the pan in the preheated oven. Bake for 10-15 minutes, or until the pork is cooked through and the filling is hot and bubbly.
Serve hot, garnished with fresh herbs if desired. Enjoy!

Caprese Salad

ingredients

Fresh mozzarella cheese. Look for soft, spongy mozzarella balls that are packed in water. ...
Basil. Only fresh leaves here! ...
Extra-virgin olive oil. ...
Freshly ground black pepper. ...
Sea salt.

Caprese salad is a great and healthy lunch option for kids. All you need are five simple ingredients to make it: peak-season tomatoes, fresh mozzarella cheese, basil leaves, extra-virgin olive oil, freshly ground black pepper and sea salt. Look for soft spongy mozzarella balls that are packed in water and make sure to only use fresh basil leaves. Finally, add a sprinkle of freshly ground black pepper and sea salt for extra flavor. Serve this delicious salad with some crusty bread or a side of your favorite pasta dish for the perfect healthy lunch! Enjoy!

Chicken Tenders

Ingredients

16 frozen breaded chicken tenders.
1/2 cup ranch salad dressing.
4 sun-dried tomato tortillas (10 inches), room temperature.
3 cups shredded lettuce.
1 can (2-1/4 ounces) sliced ripe olives, drained.
4 slices pepper Jack cheese.
Hot pepper sauce, optional.

hicken tenders are a great way to make sure the kids get their protein in their lunches! This recipe for healthy chicken tenders is easy to prepare and even more delicious.

Preheat oven to 375°F (190°C). Place frozen breaded chicken tenders on an ungreased baking sheet. Bake according to package directions.

While the chicken is baking, prepare the ranch salad dressing and spread it over each of the sun-dried tomato tortillas. Divide lettuce among the four tortillas, top with olives, cheese slices and a few drops of hot pepper sauce (optional). Wrap up like a burrito and enjoy!

Pasta With Roasted Tomatoes And Garlic

Ingredients

1 tablespoon kosher salt
8 ounces uncooked spaghetti
¼ cup extra-virgin olive oil, divided
2 pints multicolored cherry tomatoes
4 garlic cloves, thinly sliced
½ teaspoon kosher salt
¼ teaspoon freshly ground black pepper
2 ounces Parmigiano-Reggiano cheese, shaved
¼ cup small basil leaves

Turn a regular pasta dinner into something special with this delicious and healthy dish of pasta with roasted tomatoes and garlic. The combination of colors, flavors, and textures will make it an appealing meal for kids.

To make this dish, you'll need the following ingredients: 1 tablespoon kosher salt, 8 ounces uncooked spaghetti, ¼ cup extra-virgin olive oil (divided), 2 pints multicolored cherry tomatoes, 4 garlic cloves (thinly sliced), ½ teaspoon kosher salt, ¼ teaspoon freshly ground black pepper, 2 ounces Parmigiano-Reggiano cheese (shaved), and ¼ cup small basil leaves.

To start, preheat the oven to 425°F. Place the tomatoes in a single layer on a baking sheet and sprinkle with 1 tablespoon of olive oil, the sliced garlic, ½ teaspoon kosher salt, and ¼ teaspoon freshly ground black pepper. Roast for 25 minutes until the tomatoes are lightly charred and beginning to burst open.

While the tomatoes are roasting, bring a large pot of salted water to a boil and cook the spaghetti according to package directions.

When the pasta is cooked, drain it and add the remaining olive oil. Mix in the roasted tomatoes and garlic, Parmigiano-Reggiano cheese, and fresh basil leaves. Serve hot or at room temperature for an easy and delicious meal that the kids will love. Enjoy!

Chicken Alfredo Pasta

Chicken Alfredo Pasta is a classic Italian recipe that makes the perfect healthy lunch for kids. The creamy sauce, made with Parmesan and Romano cheese, is sure to be a hit with both children and adults alike.

To get started, begin by gathering your ingredients: 1 large boneless/skinless chicken breast (or 2 small ones), 6 tablespoons of salted butter (high quality is recommended), 3 cloves of garlic minced, 2 tablespoons all-purpose flour, 3 cups of half and half (half cream/half milk), ¾ cup Parmesan cheese grated, ½ cup Romano cheese grated, salt and black pepper to taste.

Once you have all the necessary ingredients, it's time to get cooking! Begin by seasoning the chicken on both sides with salt and pepper. Heat a large skillet over medium-high heat, then add 3 tablespoons of the butter. Once melted, add in the chicken and cook for 4-5 minutes per side or until cooked all the way through. Once cooked, transfer to a plate and set aside.

Next, reduce the heat to medium and add in the remaining 3 tablespoons butter. Once melted, stir in the garlic and cook for about 1 minute or until fragrant. Now, whisk in the flour and cook for an additional 1-2 minutes or until the mixture starts to lightly brown.

Then, slowly pour in the half and half while continuously whisking the mixture until fully combined. Bring the sauce to a simmer and let it cook for 4-5 minutes or until thickened, stirring occasionally. Now add in both cheeses, Parmesan and Romano, stirring until melted and fully combined.

Finally, add in the cooked chicken and any juice from the plate and stir until fully combined. Let simmer for an additional 1-2 minutes or until heated through. Serve over pasta with extra Parmesan cheese if desired. Enjoy!

This delicious Chicken Alfredo Pasta recipe is sure to be a hit with all your family and friends. It's a great way to enjoy a classic Italian dish while keeping your meal healthy and nutritious. Make it today for the perfect lunch or dinner!

Enjoy!

Creamy Mushroom Pasta

Creating delicious recipes for kids is easy to do with creamy mushroom pasta. This delicious dish makes a great meal that the whole family will enjoy. To make this delicious meal all you need are 8 ounces of fettuccine, 2 tablespoons of olive oil, ¼ pound of fresh white mushrooms (sliced), ¼ pound of fresh shiitake mushrooms (stemmed and sliced), salt and ground black pepper to taste, 2 cloves of garlic (minced), 2 fluid ounces of sherry and 1 cup of chicken stock.

To begin cooking this delicious dish, start by boiling the fettuccine in a large pot for about 8 minutes or until it's al dente. Once cooked, drain the pasta and set aside.

Next, heat a large skillet over medium-high heat and add in the olive oil. Once heated, add in the mushrooms and sauté them until they are lightly browned (about 5 minutes). After this step, season with salt and pepper to taste.

Then, add in the garlic and sauté for another minute before adding in the sherry. Allow the sherry to cook until it is almost completely evaporated. Finally, pour in the chicken stock and bring the mixture to a boil. Once all ingredients are incorporated, reduce heat to low and simmer until the sauce has thickened (about 8-10 minutes).

When the sauce is finished simmering, add in the cooked pasta and mix together until all ingredients are combined. Serve this delicious creamy mushroom pasta with a side of fresh parmesan cheese. Enjoy!

This delicious creamy mushroom pasta recipe is sure to be a hit with your kids. Its delicious flavor and simple ingredients make it an easy meal to whip up for a delicious family dinner. Enjoy!

Spaghetti Alla Putanesca

Ingredients

400 grams of spaghetti
100 grams of pitted olives
1 tablespoon salted capers
500 grams of well-ripened tomatoes or 400 grams of tomatoes in broth
2 large garlic cloves
5-6 anchovy fillets salted or in oil
1 sprig parsley
3-4 tablespoons olive oil
salt and pepper
optional: chilli pepper, fresh or dried

If you're looking for delicious recipes for kids, look no further than spaghetti alla Puttanesca. This classic Italian dish is easy to make and packed with flavour. Here's how to cook it:

Firstly, bring a large pot of salted water to a rolling boil and add the 400 grams of spaghetti. Cook until al dente, then strain and set aside.

In a large skillet over medium heat, add the 3-4 tablespoons of olive oil and two large cloves of garlic, chopped. When the garlic begins to sizzle, stir for about 30 seconds before adding anchovy fillets salted or in oil. Stir until the anchovies have dissolved into the oil.

Now you can add the pitted olives and capers, stirring for another 1-2 minutes before adding 500 grams of well-ripened tomatoes or 400 grams of tomatoes in broth. Season with salt and pepper to taste, plus chilli pepper if desired. Simmer for about 10 minutes until all the flavours have combined.

Finally, add the strained spaghetti and stir for 1-2 minutes to ensure everything is well mixed together. Serve in bowls with freshly chopped parsley as a garnish. Enjoy!

Tuna Rice Salad

Ingredients

400g of cold cooked rice.
200g of tinned tuna.
100g of sugar snap peas, halved.
1 red pepper, diced.
2 tomatoes, chopped into small chunks.
3 spring onions, finely sliced.
2 tablespoons of light mayonnaise.
Juice ½ lemon.

This Tuna Rice Salad is an easy and healthy lunch option for kids. It's a tasty combination of flavors that will be sure to please even the pickiest of eaters.

To make this delicious dish, begin by combining 400 grams of cold cooked rice, 200 grams of tinned tuna, 100 grams of sugar snap peas (halved), 1 red pepper (diced), 2 tomatoes (chopped into small chunks) and 3 spring onions (finely sliced). Drizzle with two tablespoons of light mayonnaise and squeeze ½ lemon for a zesty flavor. Mix everything together until all ingredients are well combined.

Serve this Tuna Rice Salad immediately or store it in an airtight container for up to two days. It's a perfect meal for lunch or dinner and can be enjoyed by the whole family.

Enjoy!

Thank you

We hope you enjoyed our book

As a small family company your feedback is very important to us.

Please let us know how you like our book.

www.ingramcontent.com/pod-product-compliance
Lightning Source LLC
Chambersburg PA
CBHW041150110526
44590CB00027B/4183